A Nature Walk

Walt Zabel

BALBOA
PRESS
A DIVISION OF HAY HOUSE

ISBN: 978-1-4525-5574-4 (sc)
ISBN: 978-1-4525-5575-1 (e)
Library of Congress Control Number: 2012913254

Balboa Press books may be ordered through booksellers or by contacting:

Balboa Press
A Division of Hay House
1663 Liberty Drive
Bloomington, IN 47403
www.balboapress.com
1-(877) 407-4847

Because of the dynamic nature of the Internet, any web addresses or
links contained in this book may have changed since publication and
may no longer be valid. The views expressed in this work are solely those
of the author and do not necessarily reflect the views of the publisher,
and the publisher hereby disclaims any responsibility for them.

The author of this book does not dispense medical advice or prescribe the use
of any technique as a form of treatment for physical, emotional, or medical
problems without the advice of a physician, either directly or indirectly. The
intent of the author is only to offer information of a general nature to help
you in your quest for emotional and spiritual well-being. In the event you use
any of the information in this book for yourself, which is your constitutional
right, the author and the publisher assume no responsibility for your actions.

Any people depicted in stock imagery provided by Thinkstock are
models, and such images are being used for illustrative purposes only.
Certain stock imagery © Thinkstock.

Printed in the United States of America
Balboa Press rev. date: 11/20/12

A Nature Walk

Preamble from the author

Ask yourself would you believe the message from the messenger if the message brought to you an enlightenment to the most profound of questions, but within its answer was contained a personal and emotional responsibility to change. Will you chose to awaken and become conscious of the change needed or will you remain within your slumber because of the comfort it has given you.

For fear of change we may deny the truth in favor of our chosen faith in one of the archaic belief systems that has faithfully served us. Whether born into a given faith as families pass them down, or by our own choice, it is we that chose a religious faith that serves us best, one that gives us comfort in dealing with our lives and answers to questions that have yet to be fully understood.

If we are to unite together towards a more caring condition here on earth our faiths must become flexible enough to allow us to join together in an alliance that will evolve towards that end. Blind faith is a non-evolving closed loop, having faith in a belief and belief in a chosen faith is circular. Many of us would rather spend our lives within this closed loop clinging to the comfort it has given us rather than changing the way we think. But if we are to evolve towards a more caring condition it is we that must be willing to change.

When it comes to respecting each others religion it is not religion that we should honor. It is the sincerity in the idea of a God common to us all. Although prideful of our religion there is little honor in remaining shackled to an archaic belief system that pits one faith against another to the detriment of caring for one another.

Archaic beliefs of the past existing in a world of today are clearly a growing obstacle that is keeping us apart. Religion is becoming even more stalwart as religions perceive a threat form the truth itself. Ego based many of these religions promise personal reward or favor in an after life for those who faithfully follow the teachings.

Many faith based may not accept a tangible explanation and defining of the Almighty-God. Should the Almighty become known the covenant with faith would no longer have as much personal value.

The choice is ours to embrace the struggle that comes with change and by willingly doing so move towards a more caring condition. Or remain steadfast in the archaic religions that are now at odds with each other continuing this cycle of unyielding faith that creates our own separatism. No matter change will eventually come, we can not stop evolution even in its denial. This is truly a time in our minds evolution that we are now as the butterfly beginning its struggle to break free form a chrysalis of religious faiths that have given us much comfort in our transformation.

War and or conflicts are caused by two things one or both can create a condition of unrest. Encroaching on an-others physical environment. Their land or their personal space. Encroaching on an-others mental environment. The way they think and how they believe.

We must all be allowed our dignity while evolving towards a greater awareness of this caring system in which we all exist. When it comes to our land and our beliefs we should never be forced, or use force to inflict our will on anyone. An act of force shows a lack of caring for one another and that is what creates the animosity that spawns hatred. We are all connected and must remain calm in this transition of learning. This is truly a time in history that man must learn to evolve merging together as a single caring community. Or continue to face the self induced conflict that exists because of mans own unyielding mind.

When building any lasting structure it must start with a solid foundation. If we are to create a house in which we can all live with comfort and peace, it must first be built upon a foundation of love with a structure of understanding. Within the simple poem on page thirty one rests all the tools needed for the foundation upon which we can all build a temple that awakens us each day to the existence of a more caring and understanding world. We do it by simply caring for one another.

When it comes to the
knowing of God
There is no religion to believe
There is only an
Awakening

As life is ever evolving
So must the mind
That perceives it
Our minds
Must be open
To the truth
Yet to be learned

*An open mind can evolve
towards new awareness*

*A closed mind resists
that which will change it*

We are as the infant
Discovering its own hand
As we reach out
Into the awareness
Of the larger self
That we are

Through our reverence
We gain awareness
By our consciousness
We awaken

We are creations of life
Not the creators
Of it
Therefore we need
To have reverence for it

*The Almighty is this creation
in its entirety*

*One creation of light
caring for the life within it*

The universe
Both creator and creation
Omnipotent and ubiquitous
A universal presence

All of existence
Matter energy and
All the laws
Of nature and physics

All life
As a collective intelligence
An interactive
Consuming and sustaining
Of itself

God compressed the heavens
Until they could be no more
With the force
Of creation
Exploded the core
As the core blazed into flight
The universe was filled
With its light
And the proof can be seen
In the night sky
As embers still burn
Into the nigh

On a clear night
when all the stars are
at their brightest
imagine our vision can
travel out into
the depths of the universe

As our vision reaches out
farther and farther
more and more
stars come into view
until in every direction
our vision is blocked
by their light

It is then
that we become aware
that we are now
living within the light itself

One system of light
with a sole purpose
of caring for the life within it
we are now truly
living within the light
Of God

The universe is kept in balance
through a series of caring forces
Without these forces
there would not be a universe
Even an atom has its own caring force
keeping its electrons in suspension

If not for different caring forces
suspending masses of matter
and keeping everything in balance
there would not be any suspension
Without suspension
time would not exist
Without time for life
life would not exist

The elements in the universe
are all we have
We depend on them for our survival
Through their caring forces
the elements have made up living things
and now support the life they created

This special interaction
between nonliving and living
is a gift of care
and caring is what it's all about
If not for love
life would not exist

God is Love
the highest degree of caring
contained in all of natures elements*

Omnipresence
A universal presence
All of existence
Matter energy
And all the laws
Of nature and physics
All life
As a collective intelligence
An interactive
Consuming and sustaining of itself

As we may try
Our minds will not
Totally understand our
Creation
As we live within
Creation itself
And can only reach its boundaries

This creation and all the life within it
was and is a single creation of light

We are indeed creations of the light
and from the light

We are as drops of water
each having our own form

As drops of water that return to the sea
to become one with it

Such is our soul as our body dies
so does the ego and our energy returns
to the source form which it came

Our soul is immersed
within a sea of light
within the light
is contained all the love and caring
for the collective life within it

The soul
Is an inherent energy within us
It's the connection to the source
From which we came

As the distance from God
Has its apex
So mans ego
Reaches its height
Before it falls

Both ironic and arrogant
that man thinks he can control
or that he should control
the very system that created him

The veil

Judgments are made and walls put
up to protect the child inside and
our ego stands at the entrance as
a sentinel protecting its pride

The ego has woven a mighty veil
that closes off the mind and the only
knowledge received by the child
is of an egos kind

Man's ego keeps the truth at
bay so the child may not see
blinded by the ego the child is never free

Busy with creations of its own
the ego has grown strong
and if the children don't
remove their veils
they won't have their pride very long

Zombies walking

The corpse that never walked
this way lives on the hill
in view of life as it is and as it always will

When the corpse left the cave
and stepped into the light
he molded weapons with his fear
turning him into might

Keeping back others and killing his game
the corpse entered nature looking for fame

With made up religions and
chanting his song
the corpse conquered and grew very strong

Progressing and advancing
to an industrial age
but in natures book only a page

The corpse that never walked this way
with his soul will some day pay
the corpse is ego DOA

Take advantage of position and get your fill
someday your corpse will be on the hill

From the light

From living to dead
into the light our soul is fed

We release our ego with child like fright
and return our energy back to the light

Because the ego that lives in the mind
in the light you'll never find

Ego wants

When leaders allow egos to run free
it commissions men to be
better than thee

In the spirit of God they think they live
sacrificing their nature in order to give

Exalting and glorifying
with egos in mind
they rise above their own man kind

Using man and nature for
their selfish needs
they divide one from another
as separatism breeds

Freedom of the rich leads to
the slavery of the poor
leaving the egos' wants at every door

Devils hand

Not surrendering to the nature of God
we challenge the truth
with our mental prod

Bolstering each other with
feelings of being saved
our minds became no longer enslaved

With God like egos expanded the mind
as we dominate nature for
our own man kind

Exalting the ego to a higher place
nature began falling and
so did our grace

The earth is being destroyed
by the egos of man
as our egos have become the devils hand

In denial we pray to a specious God
continuing to use our mental prod

Born again

When the truth becomes your
enemy the ego is the foe
the mental shielding in your brain
must weaken and let go

The ego surrenders to the truth
as you pray and cry
repenting and hoping to
God you'll never die

But you left the garden on your own
and in your own design
now your prayers are only
compensation for the crime

With man's ego not heaven sent
you profited from nature
with your self intent

Now you feel the pain of love lost
and are willing to be saved at any cost

You surrender to a messiah
where egos are bound
or seek within where
enlightenment is found

Life is ever lasting
Death is of the ego
It's the ego
That fears it end

*To think to act for God
is the height of mans arrogance*

If someone has hurt you
do not forget the pain
as you feel your anger

Striking back with anger
you will be the cause
of the pain

Although prideful of
our chosen religion
there is little honor
in remaining shackled
to an archaic belief system
that alienates us
to the detriment of caring
for one another

When it comes to having respect
for each others religion
it is not their faith in religion
that we honor
It is their sincerity
in the idea of a God
common to us all

What better bridge to build
Than the one in need
Spanning man to man
Through love
Over greed

Not one people
Working for another
Rather all people
Working for each other

Love is the anchor to our lives
Love is connected to our lives
by the chain of people
we care for
and in turn care for us
The more links in our chain
the deeper waters we may travel*

God
Is one religion
Becoming none